Search Engine Optimization in 2019 Made (Stupidly) Easy

Vol.8 of the Small Business Marketing Made (Stupidly) Easy Collection

by Michael Clarke

Founder, Punk Rock Marketing

Published in USA by: Punk Rock Marketing

Michael Clarke

© Copyright 2018

ISBN-13: 978-1-970119-17-6

Table of Contents

Chapter 7: Standing on the Shoulders of (Billion-Dollar) Giants 95

Chapter 8: It's About User Experience, Stupid! 106

About the Author

Michael Clarke is a former cubicle monkey turned social media marketing consultant and author.

He is also the owner of the world's most neurotic Jack Russell Terrier.

Also By Michael Clarke

TWITTER MARKETING IN 2019 MADE
(STUPIDLY) EASY

VIDEO MARKETING IN 2019 MADE
STUPIDLY EASY

FACEBOOK MARKETING IN 2019 MADE
STUPIDLY EASY

PINTEREST MARKETING IN 2019 MADE
STUPIDLY EASY

INSTAGRAM MARKETING IN 2019 MADE
STUPIDLY EASY

LINKEDIN MARKETING IN 2019 MADE
STUPIDLY EASY

EMAIL MARKETING IN 2019 MADE
STUPIDLY EASY

A Special FREE Gift for You!

If you'd like FREE instant access to my seminar "How to Make a Damn Good Living With Social Media (Even If You Hate Social Media" then head over to **PunkRockMarketing.com/Free**. (What else you gonna do? Watch another "Twilight" movie?!)

Prologue: What the Hell is SEO? (and Why You Should Care?)

It used to be so easy.

Way back when grunge music was all the rage and Mariah Carey still sang high notes that made her sound like a porpoise.

The only thing you needed to dominate the search-engine rankings with your web property was to:

1. Create a website.
2. Submit your website to a couple of ultra-shady directories.
3. Tell Yahoo what keywords you wanted to

rank for.

And things were great. (Unless you didn't do any of that stuff. Then you were screwed.)

But then a tech start-up in Mountain View, with a ridiculous name, came on the scene. And Google did more than just provide "relevant" results, or a (boring) clean interface.

It brought law to a lawless land.

"There's a New Sheriff in Town"

See, back then the Internet was like the Wild West.

If you ran an "adult" site but wanted to be seen in the search engines as a "dating" site…

…all you had to do was set up a couple of word list campaigns, optimize your meta keywords, do some spam submissions, and you were all good. (Unless you were the unsuspecting user searching for eHarmony.)

ANY website could say they were anything they

wanted.

The only way to know if a search engine result was valuable or worthwhile was to follow that result down the rabbit hole and see where it took you.

Most times, it was to a not-so-nice place.

But Google figured out that what the early World Wide Web needed more than anything else wasn't faster load times, prettier graphics or more links crammed into a single web page.

It needed a Wyatt Earp to come in and tell the good guys from the bad guys.

"What We Have Here is a Failure to Communicate"

Trouble was, how do you tell a reputable website from a disreputable one? (You know, without screening each website by hand.)

The (somewhat) elegant solution Google came up with was to create an algorithm — whose secret sauce is guarded religiously to this day — that determines which sites have "authority" (the good guys) and which do not — the not-so-good guys).

And although there are tons of factors that go into this algorithm, the basic equation is built around three factors:

1. **What YOU say your website is about** (content, keywords, domain name, alt tags, meta keywords, h1 tags, title tags, etc.)

2. **What OTHER PEOPLE say your website is about** (backlinks, directories, social mentions, social sharing, etc.)

3. **What visitors' behavior says about your website** (Bounce rate, 404 errors, time spent on site, social bookmarking, etc.)

And this whole system WOULD work just fine.

If the bad guys didn't keep dressing up like the good guys.

It Ain't Easy Being Green (or a 14 Billion-Dollar Company)

So, why should we care about Google's problems?

Well, because Google is that bratty kid who keeps threatening to "take their ball and go home" if people don't play right.

And in this case, they OWN the ball. The playground. The parking lot across the street. The entire TOWN.

There may come a day when somebody ELSE rules the Search Engine universe. (Facebook is trying its damndest. And Amazon might have the best shot of them all, with its massive media empire disguising itself as a place to buy socks.)

But let nobody fool you: Search Engine Marketing is all about getting the Google Housekeeping Seal of Approval.

And although social media is certainly the brand-new shiny thing every marketer is in love with, organic search-engine traffic still kicks major ass because:

- It's free.
- People are conditioned to TRUST Google search results.
- People searching on Google are looking for a solution to their problem NOW.

So, as we go through the various "ninja" SEO tactics in this book, and I've got quite a few in store for you, just remember Google tweaks its algorithm as often as Taylor Swift changes boyfriends. (Which is to say, a lot.)

But the core concern for Google remains the same, they don't want people to CHEAT.

They don't want people to over-optimize their sites and cut to the front of the line.

While you may be tempted to try some slightly shady Google Sniper software, or give in to the promises of some overpaid SEO "expert" who positively, absolutely guarantees you a Google page one placement RIGHT THIS INSTANT…

…follow the techniques and tips in this book.

Give the strategies outlined here some time to percolate and do their magic.

You may not get to the front of the line immediately.

But before too long, you'll be stepping over the competition. (And making a ton of money in the process.)

Chapter 1:

Everything You Know About SEO is Kinda, Sorta, Mostly Wrong

"Know the rules well, so you can break them effectively."
-Dalai Lama XIV

Okay, maybe not everything you know is wrong. But a lot.

And it's not your fault. I mean, you're busy.

Having a life. Running a business. NOT spending time in dorky SEO message boards. (Like me.)

That's because, due to Google's desire to keep the recipe to their secret sauce…you know…secret, there's a lot of speculation/fortune-telling that goes on with Search Engine Marketing. (And that even more horrible word, Search Engine Optimization.)

- Do keywords still matter?
- How much does a keyword in your domain help you?
- What's the deal with backlinks? (And how do you get good ones?)
- Can some SEO hack who called me up during business hours REALLY guarantee me to be on the first page of Google?

So, before we dig into the nitty-gritty of Search Engine Optimization, I'd like to answer some common SEO questions business owners like you have, to give you the latest findings on this ever-evolving, and somewhat complex, area of marketing:

Search Engine FAQ No. 1: Do Keywords Still Work?

Even the most web-challenged business owner knows a little something about "keywords."

Keywords are the semantic phrases that "real" people use to search for stuff. (And that Google uses to determine what a page is about.)

And it used to be that to "rank" a page for a certain term, such as "hair loss remedies," all you had to do was write an article on your website that looked something like this:

Hair loss remedies are very desirable for people who are losing their hair. Hair loss remedies come in many shapes and sizes. Propecia is one of the many successful hair loss remedies out there. It works. That's what hair loss remedies do.

And on and on and on. Obnoxious keyword stuffing at its finest.

This technique used to work. No longer. (Thank

God.)

In fact, for most ultra-competitive keyword phrases, the "main keyword" shows up about .1% of the time in the web content.

What's important now is the main phrase COUPLED WITH related phrases that are connected to the main keyword phrase. I'll show you how to do this in Chapter 4 so it doesn't look like it was done by a robot.

SEO Verdict: Don't keyword stuff. Doesn't work, and the content reads like it was written by someone who just came out of a coma.

Search Engine FAQ No. 2: Do Exact-Name Domains Still Work?

An exact domain is when you include a keyword phrase in the address of your website with something ludicrous like:

- *MartinD28Guitar.com*
- *RazorElectricGoKart.com*

- *Chapter7BankruptcyAttorney.com*

Ridiculous, right? I mean, who would do something so idiotic as create a site with that URL? (Me, it turns out. As I owned all of those.)

But those days are long gone. Google no longer gives (much) weight at all to exact-match domains.

And the advantages of a cool-sounding, branded domain, such as GoKartNinja.com or BankruptcySolutions.com, far outweigh whatever small benefit an exact-domain match might possibly give you.

Far more important are how you title individual pages or posts within a website.

So, for example, if we wanted to rank for the term "Denver Bankruptcy Attorney," then a good way to optimize that page would be: "CowboyJoe.com/Denver-Bankruptcy-Attorney."

SEO Verdict: Don't use an exact-name domain. Use your business name or some other branded name to make your site much more appealing to humans. (And, as a result, search engines.)

Search Engine FAQ No. 3: SEO is All About Backlinks, Right?

Backlinks, in case you're not up on your SEO terminology — and why should you be? — are the links that outside, external sites place on their domains that link back to your site.

And, Google weighs these very carefully in determining who are the good guys and bad guys. (They act as "votes" in separating the crap from the awesome.)

Trouble is, for years backlinking was nothing more than an arms race to mediocrity.

Whoever could get the most backlinks, and it didn't really matter where you got them from, ultimately won.

But one day, not too long ago, the sleeping Google Giant woke up and finally realized that a home's value isn't just in the drywall and thatched roof. It's the neighborhood as well.

So, hanging out in some dodgy web

neighborhoods, and getting some very skeevy backlinks not only doesn't help, but it also hurts.

The key, instead, is to go for high-quality neighborhoods. I'll show you how in Chapter 5.

SEO Verdict: Go for a few reputable backlinks. And leave the sketchy backlink neighborhoods to the spammers.

Search Engine FAQ No. 4: Can Anybody Guarantee Page One Placement on Google?

Well, they CAN guarantee all they want. But can they deliver?

Maybe.

For a little while.

But ask yourself, if the tactic is that easy, why isn't he/she doing it for their own site? (And why do you need them at all?)

There's no question that getting on the first page of a search-engine listing is VITAL. (Especially in the top 3-4 results of a page.)

But who gets on the FIRST PAGE of a SERP (Search Engine Results Page) can fluctuate wildly. (I've seen my own sites randomly move up and down over the course of a day.)

In Chapter 7, I'll share with you some cool tricks for getting your company right there on good old Page One. But just be aware, it's a position of constant flux. (And not something to worry about terribly.)

SEO Verdict: Fire that $2,500/month SEO consultant you've got on the payroll and build your SEO efforts the right way.

Chapter One Key Takeaways:

- **Keywords are still important.** (Especially in the title.) But keyword stuffing is not.

- **Exact-name domains are spammy.** Stay away. Unless you have a compelling business reason to use them.

- **A couple quality backlinks are way, way better than a bunch of trashy backlinks** from CrappyArticleDirectory.com

- **Watch out for wild claims by SEOs**, guaranteeing page one placement. (They might also have a magical elixir to sell you.)

Chapter 2:

Why Your Website Sucks at SEO (and What You Can Do About It!)

"Everything that looks too perfect is too perfect to be perfect."

-Dejan Stojanovic

In the next chapter we will talk about the actual content on your website. (You know, the stuff that gets people to do things like "buy stuff.")

But right now let's talk about the GUTS of your website. The ENGINE underneath the hood.

Or what overpriced web consultants call "site architecture." (Yeah, I think it's pretentious too.)

But often it's the way a website is organized that some of the quickest SEO fixes for a marketer can be found. (And some of the biggest gains.)

So, here are 6 Website SEO Hacks you can apply to your website (pain-free) to give you a serious SEO boost:

Website SEO Hack No.1: Make Sure Your Site is Responsive

And by responsive we mean friendly to the mobile devices out there. Because I hate to break it to you but the days of people reading your website on a desktop or laptop are going the way of the 8-track cassette.

If your site is NOT mobile-friendly and responsive to different screen sizes, you are throwing money out of your pocket.

How to make your particular website responsive

will depend on what platform your site lives on. I use WordPress and MOST website themes are responsive out-of-the-box. Same thing if your site lives on a template service such as Wix or SquareSpace.

But if your site is a custom build, made by your crazy uncle five years ago, then you might need to have a developer look your site over.

Either way, with the encroaching popularity of mobile, it's a worthwhile investment.

Website SEO Hack No. 2: Tell Google (and the World) Who You Are

This one took me a while to figure out. Google doesn't exactly come right out and tell you precisely what you need to do to make your website uber-compliant.

But one of the most important things you need to do on your website is to make clear:

1. Who you are: (The "About" page.)

2.   What your site does: ("The Terms of Service" page.)

3.   What you will never, ever do: ("The Privacy Policy" page.)

4.   How people can get a hold of you: ("The Contact Us" page.)

Now, there are lots of plugins and boilerplate templates floating around the Internet that you can use to automatically churn these out.

Don't. Use. Them.

Google wants to see original content here. They want to see your website is an authority, something closer to a magazine than some scammy website.

So here are a couple of tips:

•   **Put lots of info on the "About" Page.** Including info about everybody on your team, and all the people who write for your website. (Names and pictures are great.)

•   **Terms of Service.** This is where you tell

people what your site is about. If it's e-commerce, then you need to go into shipping procedures. If you're an affiliate, you need to be VERY CLEAR that you make money off the products you endorse. Don't be coy, be clear. Google doesn't like coy.

- **Make your privacy policy original.** Write it in your own voice. You can use other sites as a template, but don't copy. (Google hates boilerplate Privacy Policies.)

- **Include phone numbers, email addresses, names, and everything else you can think of on your "Contact Us" page.** Think of this like a masthead at a newspaper. Let people know how they can reach you.

- **Put links to all these pages in the footer of your site.** Don't make them hidden or in grayed-out text. Make them super clear.

  - This may all seem silly. It's not. It's

super-important and Google pays attention to it.

Website SEO Hack No. 3: Drink the Blog Kool-Aid

The word "blog" usually conjures up images of self-centered twenty-year-olds sharing every thought they have in their brain as they prepare dishes from a Julia Child cookbook.

But to Google a blog is a form of website content organization. And it's a content organization Google loves.

That's because the organization of a blog screams: This Sucker Gets Updated Frequently! (Which makes it easier for search engines to crawl and index your website.)

And the WordPress platform, in my not-so-humble opinion, is the best solution for this. (Head over to WordPress.com to check it out.)

It's free, there are a ton of plugins that go with

it, and Google has a stalker-ish obsession for WordPress.

So, think about moving your static HTML website over to a blog format.

If you have ZERO technical skills, head over to contractor websites such as Upwork and find a developer to do it for you on the QUICK and CHEAP.

Website SEO Hack No. 4: May All Your URLs Be Pretty

And by "pretty" I mean something that humans can understand. And doesn't look like a robot set it up.

For example, let's say I want to create a blog post entitled "Is SEO Really Dead?"

That post's URL (the web address users see when they visit your site) could be displayed any number of these ways:

- PunkRockMarketing.com/page=5

- PunkRockMarketing.com/2019/4/sample

- PunkRockMarketing.com/PageId=874

- PunkRockMarketing.com/is-seo-really-dead

I'll let you guess which is better from an SEO and user standpoint. (Hint: It ain't the ones with numbers.)

The way to accomplish this is to set up a site permalink structure, the way your links automatically generate, so the data pulled isn't tied to a number but instead to the title of a particular page or post.

Confused, yet? Don't worry. It's easy.

- If you have your site set up in WordPress all you do is:

- Go to "settings" and click on permalinks

- Paste this bit of code into the custom structure field:

"/%category%/%postname%/" (Do

not include quotation marks)

- Save Changes
- When you create a new page or post, make sure you include the keyword in the title, and then remove all words, except for the keyword phrase, from the URL

If you have your website living on a different platform than WordPress, or you have your own DIY website installation, you may need to have a web-developer type do some tweaking. (Trust me, it'll be worth it.)

All you do is tell your developer to set up a permalink structure that includes:

- Domain.com/Category/PostName (for blog posts)
- Domain.com/Page Name (For pages)

That's it.

And this is where many small business owners STOP. But they miss out on one key aspect of page

URL structure.

When they have content optimized for a particular keyword phrase, to have a URL that contains THAT keyword…and NOTHING else.

For instance, let's say I want to create a new blog post entitled "Google SEO Tips So Simple a Caveman Could Do It." And the keyword phrase I want to optimize this post for is "Google SEO Tips." (Horribly competitive, but let's give it a whirl.)

The way most people have their site set up is that the URL of that post would be:

PunkRockMarketing.com/SEO/Google-SEO-Tips-So-Simple-A-Caveman-Could-Do-It

And they mistakenly believe because the URL CONTAINS the keyword phrase that this is ideal search engine optimization.

But this gives Google mixed messages. It tells Google your page is ABOUT the following:

- Google SEO tips

- Cavemen
- Simplicity

Too much thinking for the Google algorithm to handle.

Instead, you want to set up your links of keyword optimized content to look something like:

PunkRockMarketing.com/SEO/Google-SEO-Tips

In the next chapter we'll go over why you want to have SOME content that is keyword-focused and SOME content that is NOT.

But for now just remember this:

- **Step One:** Set up a permalink structure that organizes content by websitename.com/Category/PostName or websitename.com/PageName.
- **Step Two:** If it's a page not intended to be optimized for a keyword phrase, you're done. Hit Publish.
- **Step Three:** If the page is intended to be optimized for a keyword phrase,

remove all words that are NOT the keyword phrase and then hit publish.

Website SEO Hack No. 5: Jump on the Category Train

So in the above example (PunkRockMarketing.com/SEO/Google-SEO-Tips) you'll notice I have the phrase "SEO" before the post name of my blog post.

This is a category and search engines love categories. (Makes their job easier.)

Suppose you're a bankruptcy attorney with a website that has 10 or so how-to articles on the various forms of bankruptcy. (Some on Chapter 7, a couple on Chapter 13, maybe a couple on Chapter 11…)

And this may make total, intuitive sense to you, but it can confuse search engines as they try to determine what your website is actually ABOUT. (Search engines are as clueless as a Kardashian sometimes.)

The solution?

Create "focused" categories that organize the content on your website. This will not only boost your rankings in the search engine, but also make for a better user experience.

With Mr. Attorney here, I might come up with categories such as:

- Chapter 7 Bankruptcy
- Chapter 11 Bankruptcy
- Medical Bankruptcy
- Avoiding Bankruptcy
- Bankruptcy and Divorce
- Bankruptcy and Probate

…and so on.

Then my permalinks would look something like:

- LawyerBob.com/Medical-Bankruptcy/How-to-Survive-a-Hospital-Judgment
- LawyerBob.com/Chapter-7-

Bankruptcy/Chapter-7-Avoid

This not only streamlines your website for optimal awesomeness, as far as Google is concerned, but can also help give you an editorial framework for future articles.

Website SEO Hack No. 6: Create a Circle of Life

Don't worry. I will not ask you to sing an Elton John song. Unless you want to. (Stick with the early stuff.)

I WILL, however, advise you to have every page on your website connect (through article text or dedicated links in the sidebar or footer) to another page on your website.

The advantages are numerous:

- **It keeps users on your site longer** and increases the chance of a successful conversion.

- **It boosts the average "Time Spent"** on your site, which directly affects your search-engine rankings. (We'll go over this in Chapter 7.)

- **It provides a more satisfying user experience** for your visitors.

- **It tells Google which pages of your website are the REAL BIGGIE** authority pages on your site. (Google loves it when you make their job easier.) One way to do this is to have internal linking, where words and/or phrases in your content are linked to other pages on your site.

How do we implement this?

If you're using WordPress there are a ton of plugins, such as *WP Internal Links*, that do this automatically.

You choose a certain phrase and the destination you want that internal link to go to, and the plugin will automatically create an internal link to that page everywhere on your site that word appears.

For example, every mention of the phrase "how to find cheap flights" would link to TravelNinja.com/cheap-flights/how-to-find-cheap-flights while every mention of "last minute flights to Baltimore" would link to TravelNinja.com/last-minute-flights/last-minute-flights-to-Baltimore

There will be times, however — and we'll go over them in the next chapter — when you write content that doesn't focus on a keyword phrase. Such as content that is more opinion- or news-driven rather than how-to and instructional. ("How the New Travel Restrictions Will Affect Flight Prices")

Don't stress it. Just do the best you can by linking to another page that might provide good information for a user.

Don't worry if a couple of your pages don't have internal links. This isn't the tax code. You won't be audited if you don't follow things to the letter of the law. You just want to put best practices in place that serve you and your business.

Chapter Two Key Takeaways:

- **Pages that tell Google who you are and what you're about are important, not just vanity.** This includes your "About" page and "Contact Us" page. They legitimize your business.

- **If you haven't already, think about moving your website over to a blog framework.** It's not just a way to express your inner tortured artist, but a way to organize your content that Google prefers.

- **Set up your permalinks so they automatically become friendly URLS** when you create new content.

- **When creating content focused on a keyword, remove all words that are not part of the keyword** phrase from the URL.

- **Create categories for your website**

based on the most logical subjects of your site's content.

- **Try to have each page of website content link** to another page on your website.

Chapter 3: 5 Secrets to Kick-Ass SEO Content

"If I waited till I felt like writing, I'd never write at all."
-Anne Tyler

I hate the word content.

Not sure why, got no rational explanation for it.

It's probably all those years I spent in conference rooms — how come nobody can ever get the air conditioner to work in those? — where some advertising rep would talk on and on about the need for high-quality CONTENT…

…and how we needed to have a **content strategy** to *leverage our current content offerings* and how important it was to create a **content platform** that utilizes user-generated *interactivity*.

Ugh.

Talk like that makes content sound like government regulation, instead of, you know, words that connect with human beings.

And for years that approach worked.

Creating web content that search engines LIKED, and would be rewarded with high placement, was like following a cake recipe.

"First, we need a half a cup of long-tail keywords. Then a quarter cup of bolded H2 tags, and then top it off with four tablespoons of backlinks…"

Companies like eHow and Ezine Articles specialized in this sweatshop method, becoming factories for 300-word optimized balls of content shite.

But then Google woke up from its article-directory coma and unleashed its cute, furry animals of SEO doom in the form of the Panda and Penguin updates.

When Penguins and Pandas Attack

Today, content that boosts the SEO rankings of your website doesn't follow so much a crude SEO checklist that any knucklehead with a Warrior Forum log-in can execute…

…but rather a skill that requires actual thought, time, and the tiniest sense you know what the hell you are talking about.

So, here are my FIVE Tips for creating SEO-Friendly Content for your site:

SEO Content Tip No.1: Create Diverse Content

What do I mean by "diverse?" I mean, content that comes in different shapes and sizes. Publishing nothing but 2000-word blog posts might be noble — and tendonitis-inducing — but it's not what Google wants.

Google wants your content to be a mix of:

- Long-form written content (Over 1,000 words)
- Short-form written content (400-700 words)
- Video
- Audio
- Picture Gallery
- PowerPoint presentation
- Q&A

This isn't just good from a user experience, to help grab people in different ways, but Google sees this as a sign your site is reliable and newsworthy.

Even if it's not.

And you don't have to do every single type of content out there. Just mix it up. One week do a video, the next week do a blog post, the week after that do a podcast.

And while you're creating this mix of content you want to have:

- 75% of your content be keyword-focused

- 25% of your content NOT be keyword-focused

Why the hell would we want to do something like this?

Well, in the old days we wanted to have every single piece of content optimized for a keyword phrase. But this is now as suspicious as writing off your purchase of Starburst© candy as a tax deduction.

You want to have a mix of optimized content and non-optimized content to make your site seem natural and organic.

I know this is contrary to what all the books, blog posts, and gurus tell you. But in the long run, if you adopt this strategy, it will not only make you look good to the Googlebots but also make you more money.

SEO Content Tip No.2: Create Regular Content

How frequent should you create/publish content on your site?

Well, it will depend on the goals of your site. And how much time, energy and staff you have to devote to this endeavor. But my recommendation is to pick a schedule you can live with and STICK to it.

If you can create one piece of content a week, then pick a day of the week — Tuesdays-Thursday are good — and publish at the same time, on the same day, each week.

If you can create two pieces of content per month, then pick a day — 2nd and 4th Wednesdays — and publish at the same time, on the same day, each week.

Google favors sites that have a regular posting schedule. Makes them look more professionally and journalist-y.

They do not favor the "cram for the exam the

night before" approach. If you get inspired over the weekend, and write four blog posts, don't think you should publish them all at once because you think Google will reward you. Far better to space those out and schedule them over the course of your regular publishing schedule.

SEO Content Tip No. 3: Create Content for a Native Speaker

It sounds simple, but you'd be absolutely shocked how many business owners are still trucking in lousy outsourced content from overseas to fill their website.

Problem is: Google is getting great at detecting content whose syntax is (slightly) off.

Note: Syntax is just a fancy word for how words are arranged. Bad syntax is one of the first tip-offs that content is written by somebody for whom English is not a first language.

Not only are you wasting money with your newfound international content pipeline, but it's got a great shot of actually getting your site banished from the most-favored SEO nation status.

So, if you're not a great writer yourself, find somebody on your team who likes to write. (Or look for an unemployed college graduate in your hometown. God knows there's a ton lying around.)

SEO Content Tip No. 4: Create Content That Solves People's Problems

I work with business owners all the time who get stuck about what content to publish on their site.

And I ask them the same question: "What do you KNOW that could save somebody pain, time or money?"

People LOVE insider tips. Cheat sheets. Quick guides.

Anything that will save them the trouble of having to go and learn the damn thing, your website should talk about.

Some of my favorite content subjects include:

- **Q&As** ("Car Buying Q&A")
- **Biggest Mistakes People Make** ("5 Biggest Mistakes Brides Make on Their Wedding Day and How to Avoid Them")
- **Secrets to Achieving a Result** ("3 Secrets to Clear Skin Through Diet)
- **Steps to Solve a Problem** ("The 6 Steps to a $2,000 Tax Refund")
- **The State of the Industry** ("A State of the Union of the Cruise Ship Industry")
- **Upcoming Trends People Need to Know About** ("5 Trends Every Homeschool Parent Needs to Know About")
- **How One Unrelated Area of Life Can Teach You About Another** ("What Lindsay Lohan Can Teach You About Brand Reputation")

SEO Content Tip No. 5: Create Content With Keywords You Can Rank For

I left keywords for last, because the first five tips are way more important than which keyword you use.

Keywords won't help your blog post get shared on Facebook 329 times. Writing cool, non-sucky content will.

But there is still a function and a place for keywords. They are, after all, connected to the phrases that people use to find the information they want.

The two big mistakes small biz owners make regarding content keywords are:

- They target keywords WAY OUT of their league
- They target keywords that aren't relevant

- When targeting keywords, here is what I recommend:

- **Fire up whatever SEO keyword tool you like.** There are tons of paid options — WordTracker, SEM Rush, Moz — but I still like to use the Google Keyword Planner. It's not always accurate, but it reflects what Google thinks. (And what Google thinks is important.)

- **Type in keywords related to your business.** Put 'em all down. Anything related to your business. (Don't forget competitor brand names.)

- **Filter your results.** I like to search for keywords that get LESS than 1k searches a month and have LOW competition. This isn't an exact science. But by doing this I ensure I don't go after impossible phrases like "marketing tips" or "mindfulness" that have super-high competition. But I do target keywords that SOMEBODY is looking for.

- **Remove irrelevant phrases.** This could, depending on your business, mean removing anything with the word "free" or "cheap" or "open source." Or maybe there's just a phrase that has no relevancy for potential buyers. Even if a phrase has decent search numbers, and low competition, does not make it a good fit for your site. Remember the end goal: find people who might buy stuff from you.

Chapter Three Key Takeaways:

- **Create diverse content for your website.** Publish a mix of text (both long and short), video, audio, photo galleries — whatever you feel spreads your message the best.

- **Have 75% of your content be keyword-focused** and 25% be whatever you want.

- **Stick to a regular content schedule.** Whether 1x a week or 1x a month, keep it regular and consistent.

- **Publish web content that was written by a native speaker.** And not some spam robot.

- **Solving people's problems** will always help your SEO efforts.

- **Create keyword-focused content that actually have a shot to rank for.** Good rule of thumb: target keyword phrases that get less than 1k searches a month and have LOW competition.

Chapter 4:

Your Ultimate SEO Content Publishing Checklist

"I am free no matter what rules surround me.."
-Robert A. Heinlein

Creating killer content that addresses people's questions, solves their problems and, is centered on a potentially lucrative keyword, is just the first step to SEO content awesomeness.

Once you've got that content created, in whatever form, it's time to optimize it and get it ready for prime-time. (So, it can get discovered and make you a bazillion dollars.)

And though I'd like to tell you the following items are guaranteed to work, until Google opens their vault and shows us exactly how they rank content, we must just use experience and insight to guide our way.

Just remember no matter what tactics change in the SEO content game, one strategy will always be the same:

Search engines want to deliver relevant and non-sucky content to users. (Follow that and you can't go wrong.)

With that said, and until the day Google spills the beans, here is a checklist I heartily recommend you use to get your content as optimized as humanly possible before publishing.

Note: If you're publishing a piece of content not optimized the keyword, skip the first four items.

Checklist Item #1: Find Somebody Else to Do Most of the Items on This List

You might resist me on this one. You might think it's better for you to have your finger on every SEO pulse of your website and business.

But once you've done this checklist a few times, you'll quickly realize: "I would love to have somebody else do this crap."

So, as we go through the items think about somebody on your team — or inner circle — who these tasks might be a good fit for.

Or if you don't know anybody, visit a site like Upwork.com and find somebody you can add to the fold.

Checklist Item #2: Come Up With a Secondary Keyword

Huh? You mean I've got to have a secondary

keyword *too*? Man, this is a lot of work.

It's not that big a deal...

All you do it look over your list of approved keywords — those that are relevant, have decent search volume and have low competition — and then find another related keyword.

For example, if I'm optimizing a piece of content for the phrase "mystery writing tips," then scanning my list I might find the phrase "thriller story ideas."

Sounds like a good pair to me.

Then, just take the two phrases and paste them into a text-only document, such as Notepad or TextEdit.

After that, you're ready for...

Checklist Item #3: Fix Your Meta Data

Meta is defined as: information "about" something. In the Web world, metadata is the information on a web page that tells the search engines, and humans, what a web page is actually

ABOUT.

And it's important.

In the old days, metadata was easy to abuse. Spammy web publishers would cram the "meta keywords" field full of words they wanted to rank for, even if the page had NOTHING to do with those terms.

And though Google has tightened its policy toward metadata — meta keywords don't figure into Google's search algorithm anymore — it's still a vital part of your web page structure.

There are four areas you need to focus on in relation to metadata for each page you create:

1. Title Tags
2. Meta Description
3. Meta Keywords
4. Meta tags

Let's take these one at a time:

Title Tags: This is the phrase, or title, a visitor

sees at the top of their browser when they visit your website. Some content management systems will pull it directly from the title of a page or a blog post. But most content systems will allow you to customize this.

You want to have your main keyword phrase appear as early as possible in the title tag.

Example: "Mystery Writing Tips From the Pros" is better than "The Unique and Wonderful and Strange and Bizarre History of Mystery Writing Tips."

Meta Description: This is the short, text description that you see below the actual hyperlink, when you do a web search.

And this one is important, because humans actually see it, and it has a huge bearing on whether people will click on the result.

What you want to do in the meta description field is to get BOTH your primary keyword and your secondary keyword in there.

Example: "Want to know what mystery writing tips you can learn from your fave author? Here are tips to aid your thriller story ideas."

Meta Keywords: But wait a minute! I thought you said meta keywords weren't even used in Google's algorithm.

Yes. That's true.

But if you ever end up doing any kind of PPC (Pay-per-click) campaign with Google AdWords or Facebook or LinkedIn, then meta keywords can make a slight difference in how much you pay for your advertising. (And unless you like wasting money, optimize it now to gain benefits later on.)

The process is simple: just add your primary and secondary keywords to the meta keywords field.

Meta Tags: Okay, now I've totally confused you. "Title tags" and "Meta tags?" Who can keep this SEO stuff straight?

Don't worry. Here's which meta tags you need:

- One for your primary keyword
  ("Mystery writing tips")
- One for your secondary keyword
  ("Thriller story ideas")
- One for the category of the page or post
  ("Mystery writers")
- Any other relevant tags that tie into
  your website ("Fiction writers; Horror
  fiction; Self published authors")

Checklist Item #4: Add Keywords to Your Content

This is another area where many small biz owners trying to outfit their site with SEO goodness misstep. And that is cram their content with obvious keywords.

Example:

"Mystery writing tips are good to have when writing mysteries. Mystery writing tips come in many sizes. Which mystery writing tips are good? Read this article on mystery writing tips to find out."

Unless you're on 150mg of Thorazine, this won't resonate.

A better strategy is to make sure your keyword is included in the following:

- Primary keyword in the first paragraph and **BOLDED**
- Secondary keyword in the first three paragraphs and *ITALICIZED*
- Primary keyword used as a HEADING
- Primary keyword used in last paragraph and *ITALICIZED* (I usually do this in the form of an invitation for people to comment or respond)

Geez. Seems onerous.

Not really.

This is what it would look like in practical terms:

Which **mystery writing tips** can you learn from your favorite author? Are there any nuggets of wisdom we can glean from the pros to boost our ability to come up with compelling *thriller story ideas*?

Here are strategies every mystery writer can add to their toolbox to improve their craft and reduce their learning curve.

5 Mystery Writing Tips You Can Use Right Away (this is a heading - you indicate this by highlighting and choosing the <h2> option in your Web Editor

Pro #1: Stephen King

Stephen King always starts off each horror story by playing a Metallica CD to help get him in the mood. Which CDs help evoke a mood for you?

……..blah, blah, blah….

So, those are some of our favorite *mystery writing tips* from the pros. Do you have one or two mystery writing nuggets that you've picked up along the way? Let us know in the comments below.

What the heck does this accomplish?

By using a mix of italics, bold, and headings you

are telling Google — in different ways — what this one page is about. And by adding a secondary keyword — and italicizing it — you are putting the keyword in context with other keywords.

Google loves context.

You've also asked people for their input. Which can boost engagement and send even more social signals to Google that this is important content.

But even if nobody leaves a comment, you have done Google a favor by making it explicitly clear what this content is about. (And Google will often return the favor by sending traffic your way.)

Okay, but what do you if you do if you're publishing a video or a podcast or SlideDeck with little text?

It's okay. Breathe. Everything is going to be okay.

In that case, skip the heading. And write 3-4 sentences that describe the content you're publishing, and which includes the primary keyword (bolded and italicized) and the secondary keyword

(italicized)

This is not a pass-or-fail exam. You're just trying to make your content as optimized as possible. If doing so compromises the user experience, don't do it. Just do your best and rejoice because most people won't do this.

Checklist Item #5: Optimize Your Images

I will assume you use images in your website content. If not, I encourage you to leave the 19th-Century and join us here where people love visual stuff and have no attention span.

That said, there are a few things you can do to make your images are as SEO-friendly as possible:

- **Add a filter to your images (for stock photos only)** - If you're uploading a photo that you or somebody on your team took, then don't worry about this one. But if you are using a photo from a stock photo platform, then I recommend you throw that photo into some kind of editing tool (Canva is a great FREE tool) and change the saturation or some other visual element of the image. Doesn't have to be extreme; just a subtle filter and your photo will be seen as original by Google, instead of some cookie-cutter image you got from a stock image factory.

- **Compress your images** - Google penalizes pages and sites that have slow load times. And nothing loads slower than HUGE images. So, before you upload your image to your site, go to a place like CompressJpeg.com (it's FREE!) and compress your image to a smaller size. You'll hardly recognize the difference. But Google will and that's what's important.

- **Rename your images** - This is simple. If you're publishing a keyword piece, name the image file with the keyword, hyphens separating the words ("mystery-writing-tips"). If you're writing a non-keyword piece, then just use the title of your page, ("how-do-mystery-writers-make-money")

- **Add primary keyword to your image alt tag** - Alt tags are image attribute tags that describe what an image is about. (Used with screen readers for the blind to aid accessibility.) Not only is it a good thing to do, ethically, but it's another opportunity to tell Google what a page is about.

Chapter Four Key Takeaways:

- **Find somebody else** to do the items on this list. (Eventually.)
- **Come up with a secondary keyword.** This establishes the context of your content.
- **Optimize the metadata of your content.** This includes title tag (primary keyword), meta description (primary and secondary keywords), tags (primary and secondary keywords), and meta keywords (Primary and secondary keywords)
- **Add keywords to your content.** Aim for primary keyword (Bolded) in the first paragraph, secondary keyword (italicized) in the first three paragraphs, primary keyword as <h2> heading, and primary keyword (italicized) in last paragraph.

- **Optimize your images.** This means compressing them to a smaller size, adding a filter (to ensure originality) and adding a primary keyword in the ALT tag.

Chapter 5:

How to Get Backlinks That Don't Suck

"It is better to be alone than in bad company."
-George Washington

Ah, yes. Backlinks. The hard-earned currency that makes the SEO world go round.

Contrary to popular opinion, backlinks — which are nothing more than external websites linking back to your website — are still a super-vital part of search engine optimization.

It's just that Google has systematically closed down a lot of the counterfeit backlink shops...

…making it much harder to get good quality backlinks. (And, as a result, making them much more valuable.)

"We Don't Need No Stinkin' Backlinks!"

There was a time, not too long ago, when you could buy some automated software, named something ridiculous like Google Annihilator or Article Spinner Samurai Mojo, to help you rack up thousands of "targeted" backlinks to your site in just 24 hours.

Say, you wanted your site to rank for the phrase "Pool Cleaner Phoenix."

Well, the old way to do business would be to hire some poor outsourcer, who knows nothing about pool cleaners (or Phoenix), to write a crappy 300-word article for you…

…which you, or your SEO team, would then put into your new software to "spin" 1,200 times —

don't get me started on "article spinning" — which would then be "published" on a bunch of other crappy websites that only search engines ever visit...

...in the hope that the anchor text — the exact hyperlinked phrase that points back to your website — would help boost your website in the rankings.

And, it became a huge backlinks arms race, where dueling SEO strategists tried to find the latest article marketing ballistic missile to crush the competition.

But Google did two things to turn this equation upside-down:

1. They reduced the value of anchor text keywords.
2. They penalized websites for having too many backlinks from crappy Internet neighborhoods.

"You'll Never Find a More Wretched Hive of Scum and Villainy"

For many marketers, these two changes alone destroyed years of SEO effort and created a chaotic environment of search-engine confusion.

So, what do we do now?

How do we create valuable backlinks without, you know, begging and pleading every website we know to link back to us?

Fear not!

Here are FIVE Ways to Build Backlinks that are awesome, effective and will (probably) last FOREVER:

Ethical Backlink Method No. 1: Guest Blogging

This is probably my favorite form of backlinking right now.

Here's how it works:

1. You approach a blog owner who's in a similar field as yours.
2. Ask them if they'd like free content. (They will say yes. Trust me.)
3. Write killer content.
4. Specify where on your website you'd like to be linked back to, along with a brief call-to-action about the cool, awesome free thing you are giving away. (Or special offer you've got going.)

Not only is this a totally fair and equitable way to build a backlink, but it can put your brand in front of an entirely new (and qualified) audience.

Sure, it may seem like work. (Because, you know, writing is like…hard.)

But if you have absolutely no idea what to write about, just do a Q&A in your knowledge wheelhouse. (People will appreciate those more than anything else you'll do.)

So, how do I find guest-blogging opportunities?

I use good old Google and do the following

searches: (replace [keyword] with your particular area of expertise)

- "Write for us" [keyword]
- "Become a contributor" [keyword]
- "Submit guest post" [keyword]
- "Bloggers wanted" [keyword]
- "Becoming a contributor" [keyword]

You can either bookmark these searches or set them up as Google Alerts so you can get the latest results emailed to you. Don't get much easier than that.

Ethical Backlink Method No. 2: Blog Commenting

There's a lot of misinformation about blog commenting. Many people will preach that you have to be the FIRST person to comment on a blog post to get any backlink love. (Not so.)

Or you have to write a dissertation-length

comment to get any traction from it. (Not so.)

But it helps if you know what you're doing, and not be a total spambot.

So, here is my step-by-step process for blog commenting:

1. Choose 4-6 high-traffic blogs in your general industry. (Not competitors.)

2. Sign up for the RSS feeds of those blogs. (These are the orange icons, with the three lines next to them, you'll usually find on the blog home page.)

3. Check your RSS Feed Reader, such as Feedly, to find out when new blog posts are published.

4. When a new blog post is published, head over to the post location and make a decent/interesting comment that is moderately long, couple sentences, replies to the first commenter, if that isn't you, mentions the blogger by name (super important!) and something BESIDES "Nice

post" or "Good point," and include a link to your website.

5. Use a pinging service, such as PingOMatic or Pingler, to "ping" the URL of your comment. (All you have to do is enter the URL and click "ping.")

Doing just 2-3 of these a week will boost the backlink awesomeness of your website.

Ethical Backlink Method No. 3: Forums/Message Board Commenting

Message boards can be tricky. They can be a great way to find new customers and promote your business to a whole new audience.

They can also be an incredible time suck, and a great way to induce an anxiety attack as you deal with bitter, angry forum trolls.

So, here's how to tread carefully and get the most out of forum backlinks:

1. Choose 2-3 message boards where your customers might hang out. Any more than that and you'll totally get overwhelmed. (BoardReader.com is a great resource for this.)

2. Create a profile that includes a link back to your site and a call to action that promises something FREE and COOL in your profile signature. (Example: "For a FREE Carpet Cleaning Business Guide head over to...")

3. Comply with forum rules. Some profile signatures will allow HTML, and some won't. You must read their terms of service to find out what you can and can't do.

4. Commit to making three contributions in each board a week. (Reply, question, or new thread.)

5. For the first three weeks, just reply to other people's threads. Don't promote. Don't appear as a know-it-all.

6. After a couple of weeks of feeling out the

vibe, throw in an occasional "Hey, if you want to check out my cool free thing here…"

7. Be helpful, be cool, be funny. (If you're funny.)

Most people are irrational and/or too sales-y in forums. By being different you'll stand out big time! (And you'll get a ton of traffic from the forum.)

Ethical Backlink Method No. 4: Article Marketing

Most people will tell you the whole article marketing thing doesn't work anymore.

Most people would be wrong.

It's true that the whole article marketing thing, where you publish articles in directories for the sole reason of a backlink to your site, got thoroughly abused by the spammer faction.

But with Google's clampdown, it has filtered out a bunch of the knuckleheads and left room for "normal" marketers like us.

So, here's where I make article marketing worth the considerable time and effort it takes:

- **Choose 1-2 article directories to focus on and don't worry about the rest.** I like EzineArticles and HubPages. But by the time I finish typing this sentence there may be another one popping up.

- **Publish unique articles on each article directory site.** Not just "spun" article junk. (These are great opportunities for interns to show their worth.)

- **Don't fuss with anchor text.** Anchor text is where you link a keyword to a page optimized for that keyword, such as "frisbee golf supplies" being linked to a page about "frisbee golf supplies." It's not that valuable and it's an easy way to get caught in the spam ring. Instead, just

link back with your web address.
Example: For more information on cool
ways to waste time check out
FrisbeeGolf101.com.

- **Try to include two different versions
  of your keyword in the title of your
  article.** Example: Hummingbird
  Feeders - Everything You Need to Buy
  a Hummingbird Feeder. Title tags are
  still a huge part of optimization for
  these directories.

- **Use keywords, but don't over-do it.**
  The knuckleheads do this. You are not a
  knucklehead. (Or at least not anymore.)

Ethical Backlink Method No. 5: User Profiles

In the next chapter, we will dig deep into the
morass of social media backlinking. (It's a strange
little world.)

But for now, just know this: Every SINGLE social network or forum or user group or…whatever…you sign up for, make sure there is a link in your profile back to your website.

Not only is it a cheap, easy way to get a bit of traffic. But it's also a cheap, easy to get down-and-dirty SEO juice.

And for many tools like Twitter, GooglePlus and Pinterest, it's possible that your one profile link will be included in numerous lists, directories, and compilations that will bring in backlinks long after you're done creating them.

Chapter Five Key Takeaways:

- **Offer to do guest blogging** for notable websites in your niche.

- **Set up RSS feed alerts to help you leave comments in related blogs.** (Don't forget to mention the author's name and respond to the first commenter.)

- **Choose 2-3 forums to frequent** and become an active member. (Along with an infrequent promoter.)

- **Dip your toe into article marketing.** Choose one or two directories to focus on and always post unique content.

- **Make sure every social media profile** you create has a link back to your website.

Chapter 6:

What Social Media Can – And Can't – Do For Your SEO

"The best way to engage honestly with the marketplace is to never use the words 'engage,' 'honestly,' or marketplace."
-Jeffrey Zeldman

Google didn't want to do it.

They didn't want to use likes, shares, retweets, pins, etc. — what are called "social signals" in the biz — as part of their search algorithm.

And for years, they resisted any method that might reward Facebook, their biggest and most hated rival.

(If you think the two companies aren't at odds, look where Facebook is poaching most of its talent from. It's Google.)

But then Google was forced into a corner.

Once they got rid of that whole spammy backlink culture, they had to find some alternate ways to determine who's an expert author and who is just some schlocky content spam artist.

And the answer was staring them right in the social-sharing face.

Fact and Fiction About Social Media SEO

So, there's what we know, there's what we think we know, and then there's what Google tells us about SEO.

Google is very cagey about which social signals actually help your website's SEO rankings. They don't want to create the same spammy culture they had with backlinks by giving away the secret social signal recipe.

But according to SearchMetrics, there are five different social media factors that absolutely (no doubt) affect a web page's SEO. They are:

1. The # of people who like your Facebook Page
2. The # of likes for a specific post that contains a link to your site
3. The # of Facebook shares of that post
4. The # of Twitter followers you have
5. The # of retweets of a post that contains a link to your site

Does this mean Facebook and Twitter are the ONLY social media networks that affect SEO?

Heck no, techno! (As my twelve-year-old cousin would say.)

What this REALLY means is, after years of denying it, Google is finally admitting that all of this social stuff really makes a difference.

(And will only continue to become more and

more important as Google refines this some more.)

So, keeping in mind this is still an evolving method, here's my FIVE-Step Process for Using Social Media to crush your competition with SEO:

Social SEO Step No. 1: Sign Up for (Almost) All the Major Social Networks

What are the major ones? Well, my very unofficial action list would be:

- **GooglePlus:** I know you never use Google Plus. Nobody does. (And they're doing away with their personal profiles, so there's that.) But Google still allows company profiles. And they reward GooglePlus-endorsed content with SEO juice.

  - **Twitter Account:** This is probably the easiest social network to use for SEO. A must-have.

  - **Create a Facebook Fan Page:** No-brainer here. You SHOULD have a Facebook Marketing plan. If not, do it

NOW!

- **LinkedIn Company Page:** This is overlooked by many marketers.
- Much to their peril.
- **Create a YouTube Channel:** Google owns YouTube. 'Nuff said.
- **Pinterest:** Google loves Pinterest. It's like the girl in a love triangle, where Facebook and Google fight over the affections of Pinterest all the time. This is a gut feeling, but I think Google really wants to use Pinterest as a jumping-off point for creating a visual search of the web. (Could be wrong, but I don't think so.)
- **Instagram:** Instagram is like Pinterest, but with more ab selfies and LESS pictures of shoes.
- **Whichever other ones you enjoy:** If you like, you can also do StumbleUpon and Tumblr or whatever other ones

you're interested in. But if you hate social media, as much as I do, then just stick with the ones you like.

Social SEO Step No. 2: Optimize Your Profiles With Keywords

We talked about adding links back to your site in all the profiles you create.

But it's also important to get all those awesome keywords in social network profile spots, such as:

- A keyword as the name of your YouTube channel.
- Right after your website link in your Facebook Fan Page "ABOUT" section.
- Your Twitter Bio section.
- Your LinkedIn Company "ABOUT" section.
- Your Pinterest company info, and in all of your Pinboard captions.
- Your Instagram profile description.

Social SEO Step No. 3: Build a Tribe

So, there's no question that retweets and Facebook likes and shares, and all that other social-media goodness, makes a difference in your content's SEO.

But before you promote your content, it's a good idea to build up the audience that you'd like to eventually add into your marketing funnel.

Now, I don't expect you to be a social media rock star in all the different networks, but if time is short, then I would spend most of my time working on these three that can have a real impact on your business:

- Your # of Twitter Followers
- Your # of Facebook Fans
- Your # of YouTube Channel Subscribers

Of all three, my favorite is the YouTube channel subscribers. This is because each time you upload a new video, your subscribers get an automated email update. (I'll take that over any old Tumblr ping any day.)

Step No. 4: Promote Your Content and Ask for Shares

Okay, finally! We're going to share our stuff. Here's how I do it:

Day 1: Tweet my content. This gets it indexed in the search engines pretty fast. I also ask for a retweet to hopefully get it shared quickly.

Day 2: Post my content on my Facebook page and put a question at the end to get people commenting and talking about it. I also ask for a Facebook Like.

Day 3: Add the content to my Google Plus profile.

Day 4: If it's a text article, I usually read it aloud and record it as a video and upload it to YouTube (with link back to the original blog post.) I also ask for a like or channel subscription at the end of the video.

Day 5: Upload image of post on Pinterest, with link back to the original blog post. (Set it up so it automatically does the same on Instagram.)

Day 6: Post link to blog post in status update of LinkedIn profile and my Company page. (And post link in any relevant LinkedIn groups I belong to who might find it interesting.)

Quick Note: If the content you're sharing is a video, and video is mucho awesome for sharing, then be sure to upload your video separately to your Facebook page.

Facebook heavily favors its own videos over the

ones its rival has on YouTube. (Funny, huh?) So play to their vanity, and you'll be rewarded with better placement in the good old Facebook feed. (Which will lead to increasingly more sharing.)

Chapter Six Key Takeaways:

- **Concentrate on the big social networks:** LinkedIn, Twitter, GooglePlus, Facebook, YouTube and Pinterest

- **Don't forget to add keywords in** all your social media profiles.

- **Link your blog content to your GooglePlus account** to get a thumbnail in the search results, and an extra SEO boost from Google.

- **Build a following by focusing** on Facebook fans, Twitter followers and YouTube subscribers.

- **Promote your blog/website content by following this simple 6-day promotional system:** Tweet, Facebook share, Add to GooglePlus, Turn text article into YouTube video, Upload image of post to Pinterest, Post link on

LinkedIn company page and LinkedIn groups.

Chapter 7:

Standing on the Shoulders of (Billion-Dollar) Giants

"Authority without wisdom is like an axe without an edge, fitter to bruise than polish."

-Anne Bradstreet

And now for something completely different...

We've talked a lot about creating search-engine friendly content that humans will actually read and respond to.

We've also talked about how to acquire quality backlinks that aren't spammy and will stand the test of (SEO) time.

But in this chapter, we're going to think **outside the box**.

We will build little islands of SEO awesomeness, and "borrow" credibility from the biggest media platforms in the world, that will not only help your SEO effort and lead-generation campaigns…

…but put your business in a vastly better position for years to come.

The Website is Dead, Long Live the Website

It's hard to predict what the web will look like in the future.

Will we still be blogging?

Or tweeting?

Or setting up WordPress sites with pretty backgrounds? (Hard to say.)

But I'm damn sure we'll still be:

- Buying books (Amazon)
- Listening to music (iTunes)

- Watching videos (YouTube)
- Sharing photos (Pinterest)
- Connecting with friends (Facebook)

…and probably doing all of it on our phone, or the microchip inside our brain, as we ignore the humans sitting next to us.

The cool part for us as marketers is: As hard as it is to get our own site ranked for the choice keywords that move the needle in our business…

…it's SUPREMELY SIMPLE to get one of big-platform entities ranked for that very same keyword. (As long as we know what we're doing.)

So, here are my Top FOUR Ways to Use the Big Media Platforms for our own nefarious SEO means:

SEO Platform Step No. 1: Create an SEO-Friendly Facebook Fan Page (or Two)

Google hates Facebook. But they also respect them. (They kinda have to.)

And one sure sign of respect is how Facebook Fan Pages, not profiles, can show up supremely high in search-engine results.

Now, it's important to clarify that status updates are not (currently) indexed by Google, so stuffing keywords in your next status update won't do any good.

But having a keyword-friendly name of your page can do absolute wonders. (Along with keywords in the "ABOUT" section, mission statement, and page description.)

So, what do you do if you already have a Facebook fan page that is named after your company or brand?

Well, create another Facebook page. (There's no limit to the number of pages you can have.)

One technique is to break your business into different areas of focus and have a Facebook page for each of those areas.

Say, you were a dentist in the Seattle area. Well, maybe you have a general practice, but then you also have a sub-specialty just for kids.

Then create one Facebook page that is "Seattle Dentist 101," but then another that is "Seattle Dentist for Kids." (Or whatever that keyword may be.)

Don't worry if it sounds like a lot of work. You don't have to do all of your primary social activity here.

Just update it a couple times a week and have clear calls-to-action for how people can get more information about you.

SEO Platform Step No. 2: Get in the News

As much as Google HATES Facebook, they love press releases. (Which is weird, as most press releases I come across totally suck.)

I suppose Google sees them as somewhat reputable, or perhaps they (mistakenly) believe that spammers won't go to the trouble of creating press releases about things that are lame and totally useless.

Either way, sending out a keyword-focused press release can be an absolutely awesome way to boost the SEO of your website and get a ton of extra traffic. (I continue to get traffic from press releases I sent out years ago.)

What do you send out a press release on? Well, almost anything you want.

New products, new services, new company announcements…some people I know even do it for each new blog post. (I wouldn't go that far.)

If you've got a big budget, then you can go for something like PR Web. A release there will cost you about $200-$250.

But I prefer WebWire because they're good, they're cheap, and press releases there work.

Don't forget to include keywords in the title, body, and footer of your press release.

As always, write a press release from the third person:

"Michael Clarke, founder of Punk Rock

Marketing, continues to show why he is the most dynamic human being that ever walked the earth…"

…NOT:

"We here at Punk Rock Marketing think Michael Clarke is wicked cool. Here's stuff we sell to prove it."

SEO Platform Step No. 3: Boring Slideshows for Fun and Profit

Okay, I gotta admit it: I hate slideshows and PowerPoint presentations. It does absolutely nothing for me.

But I am in the **minority**.

Lots of people ENJOY looking at recycled slide decks on the web, in a variety of subjects. (Maybe it gives them the takeaways of a meeting without, you know, actually attending the meeting.)

The number one player in this area on the web is SlideShare, a site that allows you to upload your PowerPoint presentations, word docs, Keynote projects, and Adobe PDF portfolios.

Not only does uploading your deck to SlideShare allow you to reach a new, unique audience — it's great for B2B stuff — but Google thinks SlideShare is just the most amazing thing around right now.

And as a result, ranks their pages very highly. (The fact they are owned by LinkedIn probably doesn't hurt either.)

I have to admit this is a rather new form of media for me, so I don't have a ton of experience with it. (For instance, I know you can insert YouTube videos in your decks. But haven't done too much of it personally.)

But I know it can get you some major SEO results fast. (And additional traffic, if you make your call-to-action cool and non-sucky.)

SEO Platform Step No. 4: Embrace Your Inner Writer

Now this may not be for everybody. Not everybody has a "book" in them.

But…if you have some expertise you'd like to share, then I highly recommend you write and self-publish a book on Amazon with a strong keyword in your title. (You are reading one now, as we speak.)

A "book" doesn't have to be 70K words. (Like most traditional publishers demand.) This book is approximately 15K words and took me four weeks to write.

But the cool thing is, you can literally "own" a very competitive keyword, not just on Amazon but on Google, with a good book that helps solve people's problems.

Don't forget to include a link to your website to offer people more stuff, more info.

Also, once you've published your book, you can create a "Listmania!" list, based around that keyword, with your book included amongst other books in your field.

Doing this, will give you two great CHANCES to show up on page one of Google, without a single thing added to your website.

Chapter Seven Key Takeaways:

- **Create Facebook Fan pages with keyword-based names**. Don't forget to also include keywords in the "About" and "Description" sections.

- **Send out a press release for any new announcement** or product you want a little SEO love for.

- **Take your boring PowerPoints and throw them into SlideShare** for a super quick SEO boost.

- **Write a short (ish) book**, with a keyword-based title, and self-publish it on Amazon, if you can.

Chapter 8:

It's About User Experience, Stupid!

"Truth builds trust."

- Marilyn Suttle

Google is many things.

Ambitious. Persistent. Stubborn. Pious. Bipolar.

Ruthless when it comes to exploiting user's personal data.

But its entire business model is based on:

1. Giving away cool, free tools that users become really addicted to (Gmail, Google Docs, Google search, etc.)

2. Using the data those free tools provide to serve users "relevant" ads and "helpful" search results.

3. Charge advertisers a boatload for serving those ads and search results.

It's that "relevant" and "helpful" that Google has built its entire empire on. Once users stop "trusting" Google to give them what they want…Google is toast.

When an advertiser sends a user to a crappy sales page, or some SEO guru tweaks the search results to send some user to a misleading squeeze page…

…it's Google that looks bad. (And Google doesn't like to look bad.)

Google is so desperate to make that user experience supremely awesome that they have spent TONS OF MONEY developing FREE TOOLS that website owners like you and I can use FOR FREE to make our sites informative, interesting…and capable of keeping people on our page. (Which helps boost our sales.)

Conversely, when you don't KEEP people on your site, and they quickly move on to a different site — what in the web world is called "bounce rate" — then Google has failed.

And they will bring the SEO hammer down on ya.

The shame is that Google has a ton of FREE TOOLS marketers can use to help them avoid this hammer. (And create a website that keeps users on the site longer.)

So here are the Top FIVE Free Google Tools you can use to improve your website's conversion rate, increase your site's SEO rankings, and totally rule the world:

Google Tool No. 1: Google Webmaster Tools

Webmaster Tools is like the auto mechanic for your website. They may not turn your Toyota Corolla into a Maserati, but they will have your compact sedan running the best it possibly can. (You can find it by heading over to http://google.com/webmasters/tools.)

Most website owners totally drop the ball here.

Installing Webmaster Tools requires a bit of website know-how. If you're not the webmaster of your site, then have him/her to set it up for you.

But once you've got it running you can use Webmaster Tools to:

- **Find out where your website traffic originates from.** And give you insight in creating content that addresses that region.

- **Discover which of your links are broken.** This DIRECTLY affects your search-engine rankings. Boring, but important.

- **Learn if you've accidentally blocked any of your content from the search engines.** It happens. It's your job to catch it.

- **Specify your important site links.** These are the sub-pages that show up in your search engine results, below the main page result. Very, very helpful to build out your authority.

- **Find out which of your pages are missing title tags, or non-existent meta descriptions, or have duplicate metadata!** This alone makes it worth it.

…and it sort of goes without saying. Google respects sites that have webmaster tools installed.

Google Tool No. 2: Google Analytics

This one is the Self-Help Life Coach for your website; the tool that will help take your site from mediocre and under-performing, to total website rock star. (You can find Google Analytics at http://google.com/analytics.)

While there are lots of cool things you can find out about your site, such as where in Russia most of your traffic comes from, the real "money" is found in analyzing the user experience of your website.

Setting up Google Analytics is a bit easier than Webmaster Tools. (There are even some WordPress plug-ins that do a lot of this for ya!)

But you still have to add code to your website. (Again, non-techies could use their webmaster or hire somebody over at Fiverr for a couple of bucks to do it for them.)

Once you get it up and running, here are some super-useful things you can do with Google Analytics:

- **Find out how well your squeeze page(s) convert.** (Anything below 20-25% should be tweaked.)
- **Create "goals" which determine the form of web traffic that converts best.**
- **Implement "content experiments" which allow you to split-test squeeze pages.** (This is the old Google Website

Optimizer.)

- **Discover the average time spent on your site.** (Time spent, many believe, is a big part of the Google search ranking algorithm.)

Of the above features, the MOST IMPORTANT is the TIME SPENT. Or what percentage of visitors are "bouncing" — or leaving your site within 10 seconds.

A bounce rate of 50-60% is pretty decent. Anything higher than that and you'll want to tweak your website content until it comes back down to earth.

Things you can do to counter a high "bounce rate" include:

- Adding a "recent articles" widget on the right or left side of your website's navigation.
- Adding social proof components such as Facebook Like boxes and other social

media junk to your pages.

- Inserting a picture of you or your team to add credibility and authority to your site.

- Making sure the content on your page fits what people are looking for.

And the last one, making sure your content fits your visitor's needs, is accomplished with the following three Google tools.

Google Tool No. 3: Google Trends

Google Trends is your resident hipster teenager. This lets you know what's hot, what's cool, and what people are looking for on the Internet at this very moment. (Embrace your inner hipster over at http://google.com/trends)

You can also project what will be hot and cool in the future. By viewing the history of a search term over a long period, you can find out WHEN and WHERE the sweet spot for your

particular keyword phrase is.

A phrase such as "social media marketing" is generally white-hot in January and February. Not so much in November and December.

There's another sneaky, awesome way to use Google Trends...

For instance, I can tell you when it comes to the phrase "social media marketing," the county of Bletchley in England is number two, right behind London.

Would this kind of info be helpful for something like Facebook advertising campaigns? (You frickin' bet!)

If I created a landing page that said something like: "Welcome Blethchley Social Media Pros!"...would that be more relevant than most other webpages? (Hell yeah!)

Google Tool No. 4: Google Keyword Planner

Chances are, you're probably already familiar with this tool. (It's the best FREE keyword research option out there and we talked about it in an earlier chapter. The URL is on the complicated side, so to find it just Google the phrase "Google keyword planner.")

But there's a whole lot more you can do than just find out how many times a month a particular phrase has been searched.

Here are a couple of ways I use this tool every single day:

- **Find long tail keywords that most people miss.** Most marketers don't worry about keywords below 1,000 searches a month. Big mistake. There's money in them keyword hills, and here's where you find 'em.

- **Find which keywords you SHOULD**

optimize your site for. Just throw in your website URL, and you'll find what Google thinks your site is about. (Good way to find out if you're sending out the SEO signals you truly mean to.)

- **Find good websites to advertise on.** With the Placement Tool you can put in a search term and Google will spit out a bunch of websites that are good spots to advertise on for that phrase. (Then you can contact the sites directly and get a much cheaper ad placement than Google would ever get you.)

- **Research the competition for a particular keyword.** Just because a term has high competition, doesn't mean you can't rank for it. (Just means it might take longer.)

- **Find new keywords and subjects you'd never think about exploring.** This is may be the biggest advantage. By putting in a bunch of keywords in the keyword tool, you'll automatically get a bunch of ad group ideas that may or may not have been on your radar.

It's possible to get a little lost in the Keyword Tool. Just stay focused and have fun. (Or at least as much fun as keyword research can be.)

Google Tool No. 5: Google Alerts

To keep the strained metaphor going, good-old Google Alerts is like the small-town sheriff of your website. It keeps an eye on everything, so you don't have to.

There's so much you can do with Google Alerts. (http://google.com/alerts.) Besides find out how many times your name is mentioned on the Internet.

I use Google Alerts for the following jobs:

- **Keeping track of all new external links to my site.** Simply put in "link: mydomain.com" in the alert field to set it up.

- **Finding out every time my blog or website is mentioned**, by creating an alert for my company.

- **Ensuring nobody steals my content.** This happens. Trust me. An easy way to find out if this is happening is to put a fairly large paragraph in the alert field and see what pops up.

- **Get all the latest info, news and tips in your industry.** By creating a couple of area-specific alerts you can appear way more knowledgeable and connected than you actually are. (Just create an alert for 2-3 keywords of your industry, and you're golden.)

Chapter Eight Key Takeaways:

- **Webmaster Tools can help you find broken links** in your site and tell you which of your pages need title tags and better metadata.

- **Google Analytics is an awesome/free tool** to help you track the conversion rates of your squeeze pages and find out where your website traffic is coming from. (And how best to increase that number.)

- **Search Google Trends to find "hot" topics** you can incorporate into your content and discover the best time of year for specific areas of content to focus on.

- **Use the Google Keyword Planner Tool to find long-tail keywords you can rank for,** discover advertisers you should approach with your PPC campaigns, and find out what Google thinks your site is about.

- **Employ Google Alerts to track how often your website/company is mentioned** and easily collect any third-party content in your industry you can share and/or write about.

Epilogue:

What I Learned as a Black-Hat Underground SEO

I know more about prom dresses and lower-back Celtic Tattoos than any red-blooded man you'll ever meet.

That's because my first "real" job, after my band broke up and my girlfriend kicked me out of her studio apartment, was writing hundreds of horrible SEO web content articles...

...and that includes 100 articles about tribal tattoos, and a mere 72 articles about illuminating topics such as "Discount Prom Dresses," "Gothic Prom Dresses," and that ever-controversial subject,

"Modern Prom Dresses."

And it was my job to not only create those collections of textual crap but promote them.

In the most skeevy, shady ways.

I would create numerous fake blogs, with fake profiles and fake concerns and fake links to these horrible articles. ("Hey guys, I just found this great article on *Discount Prom Dresses* that I found very helpful, and so will you.")

And then I would create additional fake profiles which would comment on these initial fake posts.

And then I would put all of this into some strange software, whose name I can't remember, that would suddenly create thousands of backlinks to these blogs and comments in a matter of minutes.

The whole thing would have been utterly ridiculous if it didn't work so well.

Really well.

Anyway…

Most of those shady techniques don't work anymore. I'm sure there are other, even shadier, techniques that have taken their place.

But there's one memory that sticks out in my mind from that time. (Besides the fact that I wrote about prom dresses for eight hours at a time.)

Every Thursday we'd have a company strategy session; this was a chance for the team to map out which niches we'd be focusing on.

At this meeting, writers, like me, would throw out different ideas for markets the company could dive into. (Examples: "Car insurance," "Autism tips," "Living Trust attorney")

And our boss would look at the results of the competition for that keyword on that first page of Google. And depending on what he saw, he would say, "Yeah, sounds good," or "Hell, no, are you insane?"

So, one time I asked him: What makes you decide whether to go into a market?

Is it the size of the company you'd have to go up against?

Or how long your competitor's domains have

been around?

He said, "No. Got nothing to do with any of that."

He told me he could compete with almost anything a competitor could throw at him:

- The number of backlinks
- The age of the domain
- The number of pages on the website

The ONE THING he hated to go up against was: Websites run by owners that actually "give a damn."

Everything else he could outmaneuver and outrank.

But when somebody was writing about something they were really passionate about, and they really, truly wanted to help people out, they produced a lot of content. Good content.

And content like that gets retweeted, liked, forwarded, commented on, shared in forums, printed out and put on the refrigerator.

And the whole **job** of SEO starts to become less and less important. And you start "ranking" for stuff, almost by accident.

So, as you dip your toe, or maybe your entire body, in the deep end of the SEO pool, and get slightly frustrated that things aren't happening overnight....

...realize there will always be some latest tool, some new gimmick that you might be tempted to throw in your toolbox.

But, if you're really passionate about your business, and write like a normal human being, then you'll have an advantage no piece of SEO software, or your competition, can compete against.

Authority.

Good luck with your SEO adventures. And if you have any questions, or you'd just like to drop me a line to let me know what you thought of this book you can contact me at michael@punkrockmarketing.com.

And if you've enjoyed this book, or even if you

didn't enjoy the book, would you be willing to leave a review?

Even a sentence or two really helps us indie authors carve out a career as a creative professional.

HEAD OVER to PunkRockMarketing.com/SEOBook to leave a review on Amazon (and enjoy truckloads of good karma):

Oh, and just one more thing…

A Special FREE Gift for You!

If you'd like FREE instant access to my seminar "How to Make a Damn Good Living With Social Media (Even If You Hate Social Media" then head over to **PunkRockMarketing.com/Free**. (What else you gonna do? Watch another "Twilight" movie?!)

not intended as business advice. Use of the programs, advice, and information contained in this book is at the sole choice and risk of the reader.

CPSIA information can be obtained
at www.ICGtesting.com
Printed in the USA
FSHW020515180319
56456FS